HISTORIC PHOTOS OF UNIVERSITY OF MICHIGAN

TEXT AND CAPTIONS BY
MICHAEL CHMURA AND CHRISTINA M. CONSOLINO

TURNER
PUBLISHING COMPANY
NASHVILLE, TENNESSEE   PADUCAH, KENTUCKY

All-American and All-Big Ten player Tom Harmon (#98) in Michigan's 40-0 victory over Ohio State in 1940. During this year, he was awarded the Big Ten Most Valuable Player and became Michigan's first Heisman Trophy winner. Harmon was considered one of the greatest halfbacks of his time. Two years later, he joined the U.S. war effort as a military pilot and received a Silver Star and Purple Heart during his service in China.

HISTORIC PHOTOS OF
UNIVERSITY OF
MICHIGAN

Turner Publishing Company
200 4th Avenue North • Suite 950   412 Broadway • P.O. Box 3101
Nashville, Tennessee 37219   Paducah, Kentucky 42002-3101
(615) 255-2665   (270) 443-0121

www.turnerpublishing.com

Historic Photos of University of Michigan

Copyright © 2007 Turner Publishing Company

Library of Congress Control Number: 2007933767

ISBN-13: 978-1-59652-401-9

Printed in the United States of America

07 08 09 10 11 12 13 14—0 9 8 7 6 5 4 3 2 1

CONTENTS

The University of Michigan Marching Band forms a Block M on the field of Michigan Stadium in 1964, under the direction of William D. Revelli, one of America's most influential college band directors. The Marching Band began in the late 1800s as a grass roots student effort and first appeared on the football field in 1898. In 1983, it was the first recipient of the Louis Sudler National Intercollegiate Marching Band Trophy, which recognizes excellence in marching bands.

ACKNOWLEDGMENTS

This volume, *Historic Photos of University of Michigan,* would not have been possible without assistance from the Bentley Historical Library, University of Michigan. It is with great thanks that we acknowledge the valuable contributions of its dedicated staff.

The photographs within this volume were chosen from the following collections of the Bentley Historical Library and are used by permission:

University of Michigan Board in Control of Intercollegiate Athletics, UM Alumni Association, the UM Athletic Department, the UM Department of Physical Education for Women, UM News and Information Services, Ivory Photo, UM Photographic Vertical File, Ann Arbor Garden Club (HS1823), James B. Angell papers (HS 1824), the papers of William Revelli, and the papers of Fielding Yost

We would also like to thank the following individuals for invaluable suggestions and feedback:

Dave Chmura
Tim Meade
Traci Parker
Mary Beth Sheehan

The Michigan Theater is considered a landmark. In this photograph from 1948, a line of people wait to view the premier of *It Happens Every Spring.* The theater opened in January 1928 and was a showplace for both live entertainment and movies in its two theaters.

PREFACE

The photographs on these pages capture the story of how the University of Michigan grew after moving from Detroit to Ann Arbor in 1837. Over the course of 170 years, the school expanded from seven students and two professors to become an internationally acclaimed institution, creating magnificent architecture, renowned hospitals, and respected research facilities where empty meadows once stood. A polio vaccine, radio-wave technology, and continuing research into peaceful, productive uses for nuclear energy are only part of the University of Michigan's proud history.

The university is frequently credited with popularizing football west of the Alleghenies. Its Wolverines and their famed coaches rushed and passed their way into the history books. One former gridiron star became a movie actor. Another rose to the office of President of the United States. Other sports created their own legends, such as basketball star Cazzie Russell and aquatic gold-medal winner Maxine "Micki" King.

The remarkable black and white photographs within this book were carefully selected from Bentley Historical Library's extensive collections. With the exception of cropping where necessary and touching up imperfections wrought by time, no other changes have been made. The focus and clarity of many images is limited to the technology of the day and the skill of the photographer who captured them. We hope they will help readers to fondly recall memories of crossing the Diag with sunlight streaming through trees, of cheering another Wolverine athletic victory, and of the instructors, classes, and students that made a difference in their lives.

Originally built in 1841 and referred to as the University Building, Mason Hall was the home of the Literary Department (later College of Literature, Science, and the Arts), the first department of the university. This picture is from around 1850, after it had been officially named Mason Hall, in honor of Michigan's first governor, Stevens T. Mason. The building provided study space and dormitories for the students, as well as classrooms for instruction.

A GREAT UNIVERSITY IS BUILT

(1850–1899)

The roots of the University of Michigan date to 1817 in the city of Detroit, when Governor of the Michigan Territory Lewis Cass signed a bill authorizing the building of Catholepistemiad (University) of Michigania. "Catholepistemiad" was a word created by former territorial Supreme Court Judge Augustus Woodward, who led the drive for a university. The name was changed to University of Michigan in 1821. In 1837, the same year Michigan became the twenty-sixth state in the Union, the school moved to Ann Arbor. There, the college began anew as a forty-acre parcel land grant upon which four buildings were erected; the structures took four years to complete.

 In September of 1841, the doors of the university opened to its first class, which consisted of only seven students instructed by two professors. The students utilized the space of what was known as the Main University Building, later named Mason Hall in honor of the first governor of the State of Michigan, Stevens T. Mason. The building consisted of a chapel, a museum, students' quarters, and recitation rooms.

Over the next few decades, under the administrations of the first four presidents of the university, immense growth occurred on the campus. The Medicine Department opened in 1850, with the Law Department following in 1859. Additional buildings were constructed to house the increasing number of students and faculty. By 1871, the university had enrolled just over 1,200 students, spread across three departments (Medicine, Law, and Literary) and had a budget of $104,000. At this time, the University of Michigan was considered the largest of its kind in the country.

Outside the microcosm of campus, the world was changing. In 1861, the Civil War broke out. The university and its students supported the Union cause. A group of students formed the University Battalion, while University President Henry Tappan agreed to perform military exercises once per month.

Electricity came to campus, lighting up the president's house by 1891. Recreation was becoming more prominent, and an interest in spectator sports grew, leading to the founding of several varsity sports in their early forms. The enfranchisement of women was reflected in campus life, evidenced by the admittance of the first woman in 1870 and the formation of the Women's League in 1890.

Courthouse Square was the site of significant civic events for the people of Ann Arbor and the university. On Sunday, April 15, 1861, the university's president, Dr. Henry Phillip Tappan, called a meeting at Courthouse Square to inform the citizens of the attack on Fort Sumter. There was a large turnout, as evidenced by the spilling of people into the street. The outcome: support of President Abraham Lincoln and the establishment of military units.

Shown from the northwest corner (State Street side) of campus is the University of Michigan as seen in 1865. In the foreground, from left to right are: the Law Building (also known as Old Haven Hall), completed in 1863; Mason Hall, built in 1841; and South College, completed in 1849. The fence that surrounded the campus was built to separate those cows owned by university faculty and those owned by citizens of Ann Arbor.

Two students lounge on a sunny day near the northwestern corner of campus around 1873. The boulder against which they rest was known as the "Pudding Stone," the "Big Stone," or the "Senior's Pet Pebble," and was placed on campus February 24, 1862, by the Class of 1862. Throughout the years, the boulder has had many homes, but in 2005 it came to rest outside the C. C. Little building, the current home of the Geology Department.

A view from the northwest corner of campus around 1873. People in horse-drawn carriages ride along State Street in front of the Law Building and University Hall. Shown behind the fence is the Class of 1862 memorial boulder.

Students enjoyed walking to class under the trees, as shown in a photograph from 1873 or 1874. The walk extended from the northwest corner, past the Law Building and University Hall towards South University.

Built in 1871 by E. S. Jenison of Chicago, University Hall is shown with its original dome in 1873. The building was constructed to connect Mason Hall and South College, thus forming a showpiece building for the University of Michigan. It provided a chapel, an auditorium, lecture rooms, and office space under a dome that rose 140 feet above the ground.

In 1855, Dr. Henry Tappan cited the need for a chemical laboratory, which was built in 1856 under the direction of architect A. J. Jordan, the first of its kind at a state university. The building was enlarged multiple times between 1861 and 1868. The photograph shown here depicts the Chemical Laboratory in 1874, after its fourth wing was added. Further additions took place in 1880, 1889, and 1901.

Sophomores sit in the grass outside University Hall in 1877. The building drew great criticism because of the size and design of the large dome, as well as the turrets—known as "pepper boxes"—at the base of the dome. University Hall underwent changes during Christmas break, 1896, with the replacement of the original dome with a smaller and less-expensive iron one. The building was demolished in 1950.

The University of Michigan Law School has historically attracted many students. Some of them are shown here studying in the library of the Law Building, which was originally housed in Old Haven Hall. The Law Library occupied the second floor of the south wing. This photograph was taken in 1877.

A university boat is led by a ladies' crew team on the Huron River around 1878–79.

The Law Building as it stood on the northwest corner of the campus, photographed between 1863 and 1893. The Regents of the university renamed the building Haven Hall, in honor of Erastus O. Haven, president of the university from 1863 to 1869. Old Haven Hall was a home not only for the Law Department (later the Law School), but also the University Chapel (until 1873), and the General Library (until 1883).

The first University of Michigan football team finished the season with a record of one win and one tie. Its captain, David N. DeTar, is shown in the back row, third from the left, in this 1879 photograph. The 1879 season was the founding season for varsity football at the university. The teams functioned without coaches until 1891.

By 1850, diagonal paths across the campus had emerged, created by students and faculty walking from corner to corner. These paths were covered with boardwalks; the major path became known as the Diag. This photograph shows a view from the old fence posts at the northwest corner of the campus in 1879. The many trees shown here were most likely planted around 1850, to lend a more formal air to the interior of the campus.

The Pavilion Hospital, shown here in 1880, was the first U.S. hospital owned and operated by a university. Adapted from a professor's house, its wooden extensions were added in 1876 and were intended to be burned down in case of an infectious disease outbreak or after a period of years to prevent such outbreaks. The hospital continued its service until 1891, when it moved to new quarters on Catherine Street.

View from the west side (State Street) of University Hall as seen in 1880, after remodeling in 1879. During the renovation, two corner turrets and the "pepper boxes" at the corners of the roof were removed. This photograph clearly highlights the original dome, standing 140 feet above the ground, which was not removed until 1896.

The first Engineering Building at the University of Michigan was known as the Scientific Blacksmith Shop. Shown here in 1882, the building was the first fireproof building constructed on campus and contained a foundry, a forge, and woodworking and machine tool shops. The building was eventually sold and moved for use as a private residence at North University and Observatory.

Interest in music began to rise in the late 1870s and '80s. The Chequamegon Band and Orchestra, shown in 1888, was a part of the growing music trend and often played at parties and concerts.

John Jacob Abel (seated) and his assistant, Archibald Muirhead, in the Pharmacology Laboratory around 1891. Abel received his Ph.B. from the university in 1883, and founded and chaired the first Department of Pharmacology in the United States at the University of Michigan in 1891. He is known for being one of the first to isolate epinephrine (adrenaline) as well as insulin in crystalline form and is often referred to as the Father of American Pharmacology.

Microtomes, much like those seen in this photograph from 1893, were used by medical students to cut biological specimens into very thin slices. These slices then allow for examination at the microscopic level. Microtomes are still widely used today.

The need for a new University of Michigan hospital became apparent by the end of the 1880s, and one was erected in 1891. It consisted of the two buildings shown here in the 1890s, the Homeopathic Department of Medicine (left), and the Allopathic Medical School (right).

Constructed between 1848 and 1850, the original Medical Building was the university's first medical building. It underwent several additions, and served as the medical school's primary instructional building, providing space for lectures, recitations, anatomical dissections, laboratories, and faculty offices until 1903. Apparent in the photograph, taken between 1870 and 1903, is the Greek Revival portico on the eastern side of the building.

Workers are shown constructing Newberry Hall between 1888 and 1891, directly across State Street from University Hall. Nearly half of the building's cost was covered by a gift of Helen H. Newberry. To recognize this support, the building was named in honor of her husband, John S. Newberry, Class of 1847. Newberry Hall was headquarters for the Students' Christian Association. The building is constructed of native fieldstone in the Romanesque style of the period.

Several students sit down for an afternoon picnic on Sunday, June 21, 1891. From left to right, the students are Katherine Durfee Hoyt, Will Conant, Augusta Durfee Flinterman, Sam Grubb, and Homer Safford. Safford received degrees from the university in 1892 and 1896 and went on to reform the Detroit Medical System and ultimately plan the new Detroit General Hospital.

The 1891 UM football team played to an overall record of 4–5. The team captain was James Van Inwagen (2nd from left, middle row), and the coach was Frank Crawford (2nd from left, bottom row). The gentleman in the suit is the manager, Royal T. Farrand. Crawford and Van Inwagen were coach and captain for one year.

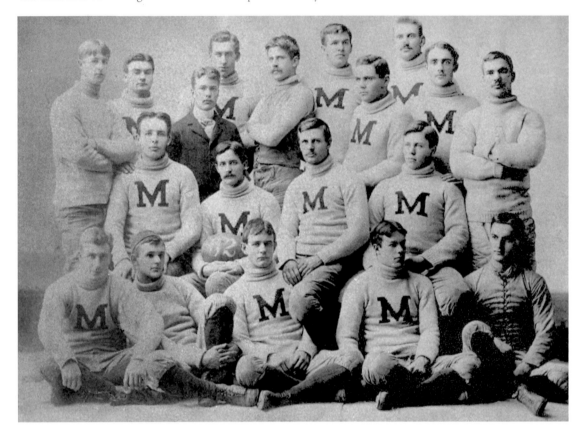

In 1889, a new building to house the Anatomical Laboratory was built in order to alleviate overcrowding within the department. The main laboratory, shown as it appeared in 1893, was on the second floor of the building. Skylights and small windows provided illumination. In this room, male medical students dissected cadavers.

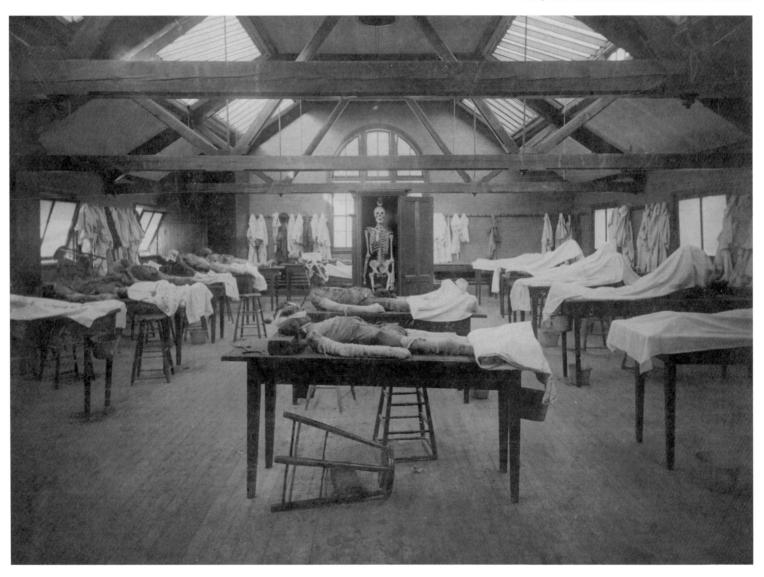

The Anatomical Laboratory Building was also home to a dissecting room for women, shown here on the first floor of the building, around 1893. Although the first woman graduated with a medical degree in 1871, the women had separate dissection rooms from the men until 1908.

A view from State Street as it appeared in the late nineteenth century. To the far right is University Hall with its original dome intact. In the center sits the Law Building, after construction of an addition with a tower.

Alice Hamilton (third row, eighth from left) and other medical school students received instruction on surgery and anatomy in amphitheaters, much like this one photographed in 1893. After receiving her medical degree from the university and undertaking graduate studies, Hamilton conducted surveys on industrially related diseases and famously investigated the effects of manufacturing explosives on those that worked with them. She is regarded as a founder of industrial toxicology.

An organic chemistry lecture, probably in the original Chemistry Building, around 1893.

Waterman Gymnasium was built in 1894 for the men to use as a physical education facility. The building was brick over a structural iron framework and included skylights. In addition to the gymnasium, the building contained an indoor running track and locker room facilities. According to an Annual President's Report, "the building shall be given up at certain times to women," as shown here in 1895.

Between 1863 and 1923 the Law Building was home to the Law School, although expanding enrollments throughout the time made two considerable remodelings necessary. In 1893, more class and lecture rooms were added, as well as a tower on the northwestern corner of the building. The building is shown here, with the Class of 1862 memorial boulder in the foreground, between 1893 and 1897.

Forrest Hall, James Baird, Bert Carr, and James Hooper (left to right) were all a part of the 1895 University of Michigan football team. Coached by William McCauley, their overall record was 8–1. Their only loss that year was to Harvard University.

The Allopathic Hospital (also called University Hospital) on Catherine Street, as seen in 1897. The hospital opened in 1891 and the building converted to the Surgical Ward in 1900. The building would ultimately become a variety of wards and centers, including the East Convalescent Ward, the Rapid Treatment Center, and the Institute for Social Research. The structure was demolished in 1965.

Louis Elbel is shown in his room at Professor Alexander Winchell's octagonal house at the end of the nineteenth century. Elbel is known for composing the march famously titled "The Victors," after the 1898 football team won its first conference championship against their toughest opponent, the Chicago Maroons. Elbel, reportedly impressed and elated, determined that the university did not have the "right" celebratory song and composed the new march on his return train to Ann Arbor.

An 1899 photograph shows University of Michigan Law School students (the "Laws") celebrating their football win over the students from the Literary College (the "Lits"). A fierce rivalry between the two groups of students stemmed from an 1894 decision of the Lits to wear academic gowns at their commencement services. The Laws opposed the idea, and thus a competition between the two groups was born.

Acquired in 1870 as a class gift, a statue of Ben Franklin stood on the west side of State Street prior to 1899. While the class thought they had purchased a bronze statue, it was actually made of pewter, which could not withstand the abuse bestowed on it by students. It was removed from the campus after Franklin's arm fell off due to expansion of concrete that had been used to fill the hollow sculpture.

A baseball game at Regents Field (originally called the Athletic Field) in 1900. The field was laid out such that both baseball and football would be accommodated by one venue. A covered grandstand that seated approximately eight hundred can be seen on the left, the north end of the field. The original grandstand, which only seated four hundred, burned in 1895.

GROWTH IN THE EARLY TWENTIETH CENTURY

(1900–1919)

The dawning of the twentieth century ushered in many changes for the university. Renovations of existing buildings and construction of new ones modified the face of the school, expanding the campus outward from its original forty acres. New structures included the West Medical Building, the West Engineering Building, the Dental Building, Alumni Memorial Hall, the Chemistry Building, Hill Auditorium, Helen Newberry Hall, the University Library, and the Michigan Union, all of which were completed between 1901 and 1920. Many of these buildings were planned by Henry B. Hutchins, successor to President James B. Angell who died in 1916.

Modifications to the campus were not entirely physical. Liberalization of curricula in the late nineteenth century brought about revisions to the entrance requirements, including a new credit system. In 1900, it became apparent to the faculty that changes in the entrance requirements again needed to be made. Fifteen high-school subjects were required of all matriculating students, with few limitations on what those subjects should be, instead of following the previous procedure of selecting courses from four lists. Adjustments to the requirements for graduation followed in 1901. These changes relaxed even further any course restrictions on students and allowed them a greater choice in their path to degree completion.

Life on campus was also influenced by numerous changes. The arrival of automobiles was new and exhilarating for students, although possession of cars was ultimately regulated in the 1920s by the administration. Recreation blossomed on the Huron River, in the newly constructed gymnasiums, and on the athletic field. In 1901, the new football coach, Fielding Yost, arrived on campus. He spent forty-one years at the university as coach and athletic director, helping establish the football program as one of the most competitive in the nation.

Perhaps the most significant change of this era was the impact World War I had on university life. The war was a disruption to students' social and academic lives. In 1916, two naval militia units comprised of students were organized and subsequently mobilized in 1917. In the fall of that year, over 1,800 students joined the ROTC, while others volunteered for the armed forces. Enrollment declined, and education took a subordinate position for students, as those currently enrolled helped with bond drives and American Red Cross activities.

Senior Swing Out was a tradition that marked the anniversary of the first wearing of the cap and gown in 1894. During this event at the beginning of the week of commencement, students would come together, sing Michigan songs, and parade to the auditorium to listen to speeches, usually given by the university president.

Charles Archibald "Archie" Hahn won the 220-yard dash against Chicago at Regents Field in 1903. Hahn studied law at the university, while also competing in track competitions. He won the 1903 Amateur Athletic Union title, and went on to compete in the 1904 St. Louis Olympic Games, where he won three gold medals. Having been born in Wisconsin, Hahn's nickname was the "Milwaukee Meteor."

The Pharmacology wing of the Chemistry Lab around 1908. After laboratories were removed from the building into the newer West Medical and Chemical buildings, the Pharmacology Department occupied the northern wings of the Chemistry Lab building.

Snow blankets the area around University Hall between 1898 and 1924. Note that the original, large dome has been replaced with a smaller, iron one, and the balustrades have been removed. The new roof and dome were designed by the Detroit architectural firm of Spice and Rohn.

Women did not participate in intercollegiate competition until 1920, but still enjoyed competitive pursuits through such avenues as field hockey, as shown in 1905. Teams consisted of women from the same class, the same sorority, or the same dormitory. Women's field hockey did not become a varsity sport until 1973.

Sports and physical education for women were still in their infancy in 1905. Many women chose to participate in "aesthetic dancing," a sort of improvisational dance, often performed around maypoles or in free-flowing draperies. Aesthetic dancing relied on characteristics of gesture and counteracted other dancing styles deemed more rigid that were popular at the time.

Students sit on the grass after an afternoon of tennis in 1905. Before this date, at which time the Women's Athletic Association was formed, tennis was one of but a few sports women enjoyed. While the men had a varsity tennis team during this time, women's tennis was considered an intramural sport until 1974.

The exterior view of the Anatomical Laboratory as it appeared between 1889 and 1903. Because demand for quality anatomy facilities grew, the Regents authorized construction of one of the first buildings dedicated to the study of anatomy in the country. Gordon W. Lloyd of Detroit was the architect. Erected on the eastern side of the central campus, south of the Old Medical Building, it was completed in 1889.

A crowd gathers in front of Ferry Field on Hoover Street between 1906 and 1909. Shown are the brick wall that surrounded three sides of the field, the front gate, and the ticket offices. During this time, a new gridiron was constructed, and Ferry Field was used solely for football games. It was later converted to an outdoor track-and-field facility.

The original General Library, photographed between 1897 and 1918, was both library and art gallery. Built in 1883, stacks were added to the south in 1898. The library was considered a campus landmark, due to its twin towers, semi-circular reading room of red brick, and the art gallery on the second floor. The 1883 portion of the building was taken down in 1918, when a new library was built, incorporating the old stacks.

The annual rush between freshman and sophomores, as photographed between 1907 and 1918. Called Push Ball, male students from each class lined up facing each other on the field, with space in between. Each class then tried to maneuver a large ball to the other side of the field without being crushed. The sport was deemed too dangerous and was eventually replaced by tug-of-war.

The cornerstone of Alumni Memorial Hall was laid in June 1908 by Judge Claudius B. Grant. Dedicated to members of the university who had served their country in the armed forces, the idea for the building actually dates back to 1864, but it wasn't until 1904 that the southwest corner of campus was secured for the site. Originally, it housed the University's art collection, moved from the library, but it has been put to many uses over the years.

Basketball was the first competitive team sport for women, beginning in 1898; this team photo is from 1908. Basketball was not considered an intercollegiate sport, so women were forced to play against teams formed in the dormitories, sororities, or at the local level. Women's basketball became a varsity sport in 1973.

The captain of the 1909 football team, Dave Allerdice. That season he made three field goals against Ohio State University, a record that stood until 1981, when it was tied. Following his years at the university, he was the football coach for University of Texas at Austin, 1911–15, where he coached to a 33–7 overall record.

The construction of the Waterman Gymnasium for men brought about the campaign to build a gymnasium for women. The building, designed by E. W. Arnold, was constructed in 1895–96, and named Barbour Gymnasium in 1898 in honor of Levi Barbour, who donated land that was ultimately sold to help finance construction. Both gymnasiums are shown here between 1902 and 1916 (Barbour on left, Waterman on right).

In 1912, football games were still played at Ferry Field. The kickoff of the last home game of that season, November 16, is shown here. The Wolverines, under Coach Fielding Yost, defeated Cornell, 20–7. As always with Michigan games, fans packed the stadium to capacity.

A view of the campus and the Diag as seen from the Engineering building located at the southeast corner, between 1908 and 1918. On the left stand the Engineering shops, while on the right is the Boiler House. Directly behind the Boiler House in this view is the Chemistry Lab.

The Barbour Gymnasium was central to all women's activities, such as this 1910 basketball game. In addition to the gym, the first floor also housed offices for the Department of Physical Education for Women and the Dean of Women. Besides physical education activities, Barbour Gymnasium was regularly used for large social occasions.

Senior women in cap and gown at Lantern Night in 1911. Lantern Night was an annual tradition and part of commencement activities. On that night, senior women passed lanterns to junior women, symbolizing the passing of another academic year.

In the early 1900s, the junior class began hosting a dance known as the Junior Hop, or J-Hop. Often celebrated in Waterman Gymnasium, J-Hops began at a local hotel called Gregory House in 1872. Note the formation of the block M by the students attending the J-Hop in 1912.

The original General Library under a blanket of snow, photographed from the north, which allows a view of the circular reading room with the art gallery on top. Students using the reading room were separated by gender. At this time, the library's bookstack capacity was 200,000 volumes. Aside from the fireproof bookstacks, the building was declared a fire hazard in 1915, the year after this picture was taken.

Groundbreaking for the new Michigan Union in 1916. The original Union
Clubhouse, shown in rear, was the renovated residence of Judge Thomas Cooley,
a member of the Law Faculty. Despite several remodelings, increasing enrollments
made a new, larger structure a necessity.

Former University President James Burrill Angell's funeral procession on April 3, 1916. The procession made its way up State Street (where this photo was taken) to North University, Washtenaw, and Geddes avenues. "Prexy Angell," as he was affectionately known, served the university for thirty-eight years and has the distinction of being Michigan's longest-serving president.

Women walk by the flagpole on campus around 1910. The flagpole was obtained in 1898 as an artifact from the 1893 World's Columbian Exposition, held in Chicago. The 164-foot flagpole was originally placed in the center of campus, near the old General Library. Upon demolition of that building, the flag was moved to the north end of the Diag.

Due to space constrictions on campus, further expansions of the old General Library were impossible. The decision was made to build a new library on the same site, retaining the old stacks. Two stacks were built at right angles to the old ones, as shown in this photograph from 1917. Later, in 1918, what remained of the old library was demolished, and construction of the new General Library began.

Fielding "Hurry Up" Yost, head football coach 1901–23 and 1925–26, buys a Liberty Bond in 1917. Under Yost, the Wolverines won ten Big Ten championships. Twenty of his players became All-Americans. In 1901–05, his teams outscored opponents 2,821 to 42. His 16–3–1 record against rival Ohio State is the best among UM football coaches. The College Football Hall of Fame describes his "Point-a-Minute" teams as the most devastating in the sport's history.

A group of students marches up Hoover Street in 1918. Ann Arbor and the University of Michigan supported President Wilson and World War I. Students became involved in naval militia units, ROTC, and the armed forces. In April 1918, the War Department asked the university to train non-college draftees as machinists, gunsmiths, blacksmiths, mechanics, and carpenters.

During World War I, divisions of the Naval Reserves were housed in Waterman Gymnasium. In this picture from 1918, a group of university students is being sworn into the Navy. Other buildings and sites were also put to use for the war effort, including Ferry Field and the Michigan Union.

A Rope Contest on Ferry Field on May 18, 1918, was part of the students' annual Spring Games.

The winner of the 1918 Spring Games was the Class of 1921, who were just freshmen at the time.

M. Thomas Murphy and Irving Kane Pond pose in 1918 alongside "Scholar," one of two statues above the entrance to the Michigan Union. Pond, who was born in Ann Arbor and received a degree from the university, was an architect of the Michigan Union. Murphy sculpted the statue, which faces Central and North campuses.

Students dance around a maypole in the spring of 1910. The maypole dance was the finale of what was commonly known as the Freshman Pageant, a part of commencement activities that occurred before the Lantern Night procession.

The Engineering shops were originally built next to the first engineering building, the Scientific Blacksmith Shop. An expansion in 1887 removed the Scientific Blacksmith Shop and left the building with a central tower, a one-story forge and foundry shop, and a west wing. In 1918, a clock and chimes were removed from the old General Library and added to the building, as shown in this photograph.

The Spring Games of 1918 included the Freshman-Sophomore Tug-of-War across the Huron River. First held in 1890, the tug-of-war could be seen on campus through the 1970s and often drew crowds as large as seven thousand. Only two rules existed: 1) Standing in more than two feet of water was not allowed; 2). The first team to pull the other into the drink was the winner.

A view from the Michigan Union tower, facing
northeast in 1919, shows from left to right
the Law Building, University Hall, University
Museum, and Alumni Memorial Hall. Behind
University Museum is the New General Library.

Originally, the southeastern Professor's House, after renovations the School of Dentistry was housed here until 1892, when the building was renovated and enlarged to be used by the School of Engineering. Shown here in 1919, the School of Engineering occupied the Old Engineering Building from 1892 until 1922.

From Campus Expansion to the Great Depression

(1920–1939)

The postwar era for the University of Michigan was oscillatory. With The Great War over, academics and research resumed their prominence as the focal points for students and faculty. In 1920, the College of Engineering was reorganized. President Marion L. Burton appealed to increase funds for research, successfully doubling the university's income. Student enrollment also increased campus-wide. Moreover, the Catherine Street hospitals maintained their reputation for excellence, resulting in the much larger University Hospital, which opened its doors in 1925.

In 1929, Alexander G. Ruthven was elected president of the university and introduced new forms of administration in an effort to better manage the school. He appointed officers to handle such items as business and financial matters, building operations, and provision of equipment. He succeeded in forming an entity that mimicked corporate counterparts.

Unfortunately, this era also harbored the Great Depression, and the university was not unaffected. The city of Ann Arbor incurred an unemployment rate of 10–15 percent, while the university instituted salary cuts and eliminated almost one hundred positions. Enrollment dropped, reaching a low in the 1933–34 academic year. The students on campus, once known for wearing the finest clothes to class, could no longer support their fancy lifestyles. Social clubs, fraternities, and sororities all suffered during the Great Depression, as memberships declined and finances dwindled.

Despite the hardship, the period was filled with optimism. New scholarships were created by the Regents to help with student financial strain. Class dances and visits by big bands such as Count Basie and Tommy Dorsey broke up the monotony. The Michigan League building for women was completed and athletic facilities were updated, including construction of the Intramural Sports Building, Yost Field House, and Michigan Stadium. New dormitories were erected, and several schools relocated to their own designated buildings, including the Law Quadrangle, the School of Architecture, and the School of Business Administration.

At the new football stadium, numerous legends were born. William D. Revelli arrived on campus as director of the Michigan Marching Band. He would invigorate the band program and thrill football spectators for almost forty years, leaving a world-renowned band program as his legacy. Running back Tom Harmon and center/linebacker Gerald Ford, Jr., would become famous, each in his own right.

On a snowy day in 1921, a photographer takes a picture of the view one would see if walking toward the West Engineering Building. The path, leading from the Diag to East University, crosses under the arch of the building. The arch is properly known as the Denison Archway but became commonly referred to as the Engin Arch.

The Martha Cook Building in 1921. Constructed in 1915 as a residence for women, it was the result of a donation from William Wilson Cook in honor of his mother, Martha Walford Cook. The building was designed by New York architects York and Sawyer and is located on the block between South University and Tappan avenues. The grounds around the building included an expansive garden and tennis court.

Women play golf in 1922, one of few sports offered to them during this time. It was not recognized as a varsity sport until 1976.

Ice hockey became a varsity sport for men during the 1922–23 season. Coach Joe Barss, standing at right, is shown with his inaugural team. A University of Michigan Medical School graduate and World War I veteran, he led his team to a 26–21–4 record over five seasons. The captain of the 1922–23 team, Kyle MacDuff, is in the back row, fourth from the left.

A southwest aerial view of the campus around 1923. In the foreground is Ferry Field, with an at-capacity crowd watching a football game's halftime show. The dome of University Hall and the tower of the University Museum are in the background. The white building at the top of the photograph is University (Old Main) Hospital.

A photograph taken from East University Avenue between 1922 and 1925 shows the West Engineering Building, designed by Mason and Kahn of Detroit and completed in 1904. In 1909–10, an extension was added to the east wing over the Naval Tank. The building was known as the New Engineering Building, but was renamed West Engineering when a new structure built across East University was named East Engineering.

The New General Library was constructed between 1916 and 1920 on the same site as the Old General Library. Four stories tall and designed by Albert Kahn, the building was much like libraries found at Harvard and University of California. The only surviving structures from the old building were the bookstacks. The North face of the library is shown here in a photo that dates from 1920–25.

The Yost Field House dedication in 1923. Constructed that same year, the field house was designed to be a home for football, baseball, basketball, and track events. It was named after the great football coach, Fielding H. Yost. The band in this photo is the Marine Band, which attended the festivities along with fifteen hundred Marines and Secretary of the Navy Edwin Denby.

A northern view of Yost Field House. It was constructed on State Street, on the east side of Ferry Field, in Italian Romanesque style. The massive structure was built with roof trusses that could support not only the roof, but also four balconies. The large size of the field house benefited the football, baseball, and track teams, which were able to practice even in the winter and early spring.

The football teams play against the Quantico Marines in this photograph from November 10, 1923. At halftime, the Marine Marching Band formed a familiar "M" with the hopes of inspiring their team to victory. The Wolverines ended up winning the game, 26–6, in front of a crowd of forty thousand at Ferry Field.

The front face of the Michigan Union around 1923. The building, finished in 1919, was considered massive compared with clubhouses used by students at other universities. The interior was also built on a large scale and included a large lobby on the first floor, several dining rooms with well-equipped kitchens, sixty sleeping rooms for alumni, and a swimming pool.

The front of East Engineering Building on East University in 1924. It was constructed due to a growth in the field of engineering and housed several branches, including aeronautical engineering, chemical and metallurgical engineering, transportation engineering, and engineering research. The large building included eleven recitation rooms, fifty-seven laboratories, thirty-one offices, three drafting rooms, seven shops, and two libraries.

A view of the Catherine Street Hospitals around 1925, before replacement by University Hospital. The large building in the foreground is the Psychopathic Hospital, while just behind it is the Surgical Ward (formerly Allopathic Hospital). At the time this photo was taken, the United States medical community recognized the Catherine Street Hospitals as the largest teaching hospital in the nation.

A picture of University Hospital taken from the Medical School in 1925. Also known as Old Main, the building was open for use in August 1925. Constructed in the shape of a double Y, University Hospital boasted ten acres of floor space and two miles of corridors. In 1931, two additional stories were added.

The former Cincinnati Reds and New York Yankees pitcher Ray Fisher was baseball coach for the Wolverines for thirty-eight years, from 1921 until 1958. He is shown here in 1925. During his tenure, the Wolverines won fifteen Big Ten Conference titles and one National Collegiate Athletic Association championship, in 1953. He led the team to an overall record of 637–294–8; nineteen of his players went on to the major leagues.

By the early 1920s, the College of Literature, Science, and the Arts needed a new home, prompting construction of James B. Angell Hall, shown here October 25, 1925. Built directly in front of University Hall, Angell Hall's designer featured a classical model with eight Doric columns and a wide expanse of steps at the facade.

Coeds swim at the Michigan Union pool around 1925. The pool, along with a library on the second floor, was originally left unfinished. Alumni and students eventually found funding for the forty thousand dollars needed to complete the pool. At this time, women were only allowed to enter the Union in the presence of a male escort and only through the North entrance.

The Freshman-Sophomore Tug-of-War across the Huron River during the Spring Games of 1926 drew a crowd to the banks of the river. A popular place for the Tug-of-War was the span of the Huron River near the Wall Street Bridge.

Football's popularity rose after the World War I, prompting UM football coach and athletic director Fielding Yost to propose the construction of a new stadium to the University Senate. A site across the railroad track from Ferry Field on Main Street was chosen. This 1926 picture shows early construction of the bleachers of Michigan Stadium. Ferry Field is in the background.

Philip Northrup, shown doing the long jump in 1927, was the individual NCAA champ in javelin (1925, 1926) and pole vault (1925). The coach of the track team during Northrup's time at the university was Stephen Farrell.

Two students, Jane Camp and Barbara Lorch, ride their bicycles on campus. Bicycles had become a popular mode of transportation for many students during the 1920s and '30s.

The Thomas Henry Simpson Memorial Institute of Medical Research is shown as it stood in 1927. The building was completed in 1926. The Institute was a gift from Mrs. Christine McDonald Simpson in memory of her husband, Thomas Henry Simpson, who had died of pernicious anemia. The building was constructed with the stipulation that it be used to investigate all aspects of pernicious anemia and help those afflicted with it.

A group of students roller skates in front of Angell Hall in 1927. During this time, student-owned automobiles were banned on campus, except for extraordinary circumstances. At one point, it is said that students decided to retaliate against the administration and turned the Diag into a roller rink.

The William L. Clements Library in 1927. Built in 1923 on South University Avenue next to the president's house, one of the original professors' houses had to be demolished to make room for it. When constructed, the West Physics Building stood to the North. The library was originally built to hold a rare book collection donated to the university by William L. Clements of Bay City, Michigan. The building still stands today.

A group of women practice archery in the late 1920s. The sport did not become a part of the Michigan Intercollegiate Athletic Association until 1952.

In 1926, the Alumni Residence at 1219 Washtenaw Avenue was purchased by the university to be used as a dormitory for women. Shown here in 1928, the building was the former residence of William D. Harriman. In 1944, the name was changed to Mary Markley House, in honor of Mary Elizabeth Butler Markley, one of the first women to graduate from UM. The building closed in 1950.

The Alexander G. Ruthven Museums Building was built when the need for natural history museum space exceeded what was available. Constructed in 1928, around the time this photo was taken, the building housed the museums of anthropology, zoology, and paleontology and the University Herbarium. The main entrance, with its doors of perforated bronze, was at the corner of North University and Washtenaw avenues. Museum Director Ruthven was also the seventh president of the university.

Funded by the Women's League of the University, the Michigan League was constructed as the women's counterpart to the men's Michigan Union. The purpose of the building was to provide a space for women's recreational, social, and cultural activities. Designed by the same architects who planned the Union, the League was opened on May 4, 1929, and is shown here in November of that year.

A football game against Harvard University at Michigan Stadium, November 9, 1929. The Wolverines won 14–12 in front of 85,042 spectators.

An aerial view of the main campus in 1930. In the foreground on the left is the Law Quadrangle. At the time of this photograph, the William W. Cook Legal Research Building at the south side of the Law Quadrangle was still under construction. In the upper right hand corner of the photograph, Old Main Hospital is visible.

Jean Paul Slusser, an instructor and graduate of the university, holds an art class in the Law Quadrangle around 1930.

Located east of the Women's Athletic Field on Observatory Street, Mosher-Jordan Halls was the first large women's dormitory at the University of Michigan. It was completed in the summer of 1930. With a capacity of 450, the building was actually two residence halls joined by a kitchen. Its name honors the first two deans of women, Eliza M. Mosher and Myra B. Jordan.

The *Daily News* editorial staff around 1930. The student-run daily publication, founded in 1890, became known during the 1930s for publishing new political and economic viewpoints, and it transitioned from just a campus newspaper to a widely read one. Now called the *Michigan Daily*, it is published five days a week during the normal academic year and weekly during the spring and summer terms. Along the rear wall are publications from other universities, such as Brown, Cornell, and Notre Dame.

Drake's Sandwich Shop faced the Diag on North University, and attracted all sorts of people, from townies to students to the Ann Arbor Police Force. In this photograph from the 1930s, signs in the windows advertise Ice Cold Buttermilk for 10¢ and Fresh Lemonade for 15¢. The shop closed in 1993.

Students enjoy a sunny stroll through campus around 1930.

Track star Eddie Tolan crossing the 200-meter-dash finish line and setting an Olympic record. Tolan competed for UM from 1929–31 and set numerous records in sprinting. At the 1932 Los Angeles Olympics, Tolan became the first African American to win two gold medals, setting Olympic records in both the 100- and 200-meter dashes.

View of the Architecture
Building around
1930, shortly after its
construction in 1928. This
building is now known
as Lorch Hall, after its
designer and the first
dean of the College of
Architecture, Emil Lorch.
The Architecture program
moved to North Campus
in 1974.

The Cook Law Quadrangle north entrance, located on South University Avenue. This photograph of the main entrance, taken around 1930, shows off the beautiful Tudor Gothic styling of the Law Quad. Built in 1924, this is one of four law buildings donated by alumnus and New York lawyer William Cook. It was designed by architects York and Sawyer.

West Engineering Building and the Denison Archway, 1921. The original plans for the West Engineering Building, designed by architects Kahn and Mason, would have blocked the diagonal walkway. Engineering Professor Charles Simeon Denison drew the arch sketch that provided the solution for the blocked path.

The Burton Memorial Tower, designed by Albert Kahn, was dedicated in 1936 in memory of President Dr. Marion LeRoy Burton (1920–25). A famous UM monument, this centralized clock tower was intended to be visible from all locations on campus. President Burton had proposed a tower to commemorate 236 members of the university's community who died in World War I, but his proposal was rejected.

Nighttime view of the Charles Baird Carillon in the Burton Memorial Tower around 1936. The carillon is the third heaviest in the world, and has fifty-five bells. The forty-foot-high bell chamber was designed to allow the sound of the carillon to carry to the greatest extent.

Students walking through the Diag around 1937. The style of dress at this time was much more formal than in later years.

124

One of the last Senior Swing Outs before the custom ended in 1934.

The Legal Research Building aglow on a snowy winter night in the late 1930s or early 1940s.

Female students in a "correctives class" in Barbour Gymnasium, 1937. A well-equipped corrective room was a part of the gymnasium, and allowed for women with temporary or permanent disabilities to participate in physical education.

This wintry photo of Angell Hall, facing State Street.

Construction of the Horace H. Rackham School of Graduate Studies in 1937. The trustees of the Horace H. Rackham and Mary A. Rackham Fund gave the building, along with a generous endowment, to the university. The building was dedicated in June 1938.

Paul Kromer (#83) opens a hole for his "Touchdown Twin" Tom Harmon (#98) in their 14-0 victory over Illinois in 1938. Kromer and Harmon sport the winged helmet design, which debuted that season at the opener against Michigan State. Coach Herbert O. "Fritz" Crisler had the design painted on the helmet in maize and blue. The design has come to represent University of Michigan football, although other Michigan teams have adopted the pattern as well.

Students study in the
formally decorated
Rackham study hall, 1939.

Bill Watson vaults over the high jump for the track team in the late 1930s. Known as "Big Bill," he was the first black athlete to be elected captain of the Michigan track team. The Wolverines won Big Ten team championships each year of Watson's tenure, when he was also the individual winner of the long jump. He was inducted into the UM Hall of Honor posthumously in 1982.

Bennie Oosterbaan received the Western Conference Medal for both academic and athletic excellence and was honored as an All-American five times while playing for Michigan: three times for football (1925, 1926, 1927) and twice for basketball (1927, 1928). In 1928, he led the basketball conference in scoring with 178 points. Oosterbaan also served as basketball coach 1939–46 and coached the Wolverine football team 1948–58. He was Coach of the Year in 1948, when his team shared the National Championship with Notre Dame.

Wartime Advances in Science and Law

(1940–1949)

Campus life altered again as students rose to support the Second World War. Students volunteered in University Hospital, sponsored war bond sales, and led scrap metal drives. Military groups began to occupy the recently completed buildings of the 1920s and 1930s. Reluctant to allow the university to be overrun by military installations, President Alexander Ruthven offered it to the military as a place for professional and technical training, thereby protecting the school's academic character while still aiding the war effort. The Army, recognizing a need to train large numbers of professionals for war, established a new concept, The Judge Advocate General's School (TJAGSA) for military lawyers, at the University of Michigan in September 1942. With wartime law-school enrollment plummeting to seventy students, the arrangement was ideal. The JAGSA graduated nearly twenty-five hundred students by war's end.

Several key scientific advances emanated from the university's wartime partnership with the government, including the formulation of the influenza vaccine by School of Health Professor Thomas Francis. Research in radar jamming and radio proximity detonation helped develop the Variable Time (VT) fuse, which used radio waves to "sense" when an explosion would cause maximum damage. VT fuses were credited with fifty-one percent of anti-aircraft hits on Axis airplanes.

University enrollment spiked from 12,000 at war's end to 19,000 by the fall of 1946 as the veterans poured in, rapidly creating the need for more housing and new academic buildings. Temporary veteran's housing was constructed near central campus while work was being completed on the more permanent University Terrace married housing. A new dormitory for women, an addition to East Quad, the School of Business Administration, the Administration Building, and a Food Service Building were other additions to campus in the expansion of 1948–1949.

Students of the post-war campus were more somber and studious than their pre-war counterparts. A group of those students, along with faculty and regents, formed the War Memorial Committee, which was dedicated to the exploration of peaceful uses for atomic power. This group formed the idea of the Michigan Memorial Phoenix Project as a living monument to honor the more than five hundred members of the university killed in the war. The Phoenix Memorial Laboratory continues its mission of research into peaceful uses for nuclear energy.

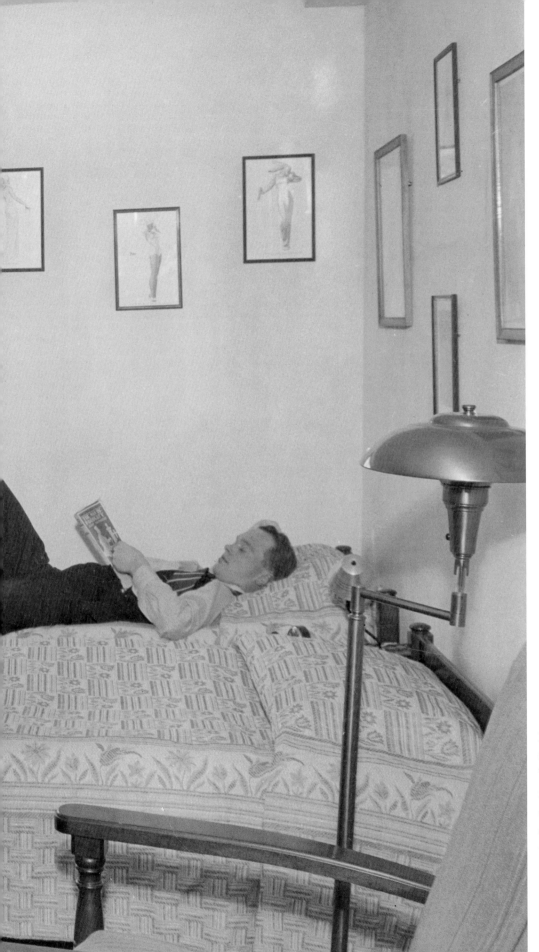

Male students lounging in a West Quadrangle dorm room around 1940. West Quad played an important role in housing World War II naval enlistees who referred to the building as "the ship." The dorm was returned to normal student use in 1946.

A boy peers through the gate to Ferry Field. Albert Kahn designed the gate and surrounding brick wall containing ticket windows. Dexter M. Ferry, Detroit businessman and philanthropist, gave the university twenty acres for athletic use and funds for the gate.

Stockwell Hall around 1940. Set on the Hill, this all-female dormitory overlooked Palmer Field, the women's physical education grounds. Stockwell Hall was named after Madelon Louisa Stockwell, the first woman admitted to the university, in 1870. Stockwell Hall remains an all-female residence.

Mason Hall, shown here in 1940, about a decade before it was removed, along with South College. The new Mason Hall was built in 1952.

Members of the Ski Club enjoy a wintry day in Michigan as they pose near
the bus during the 1940s.

The Michigan League Garden (1940) framed by the League's North and South wing. The garden is bordered on the street by a tall, brick wall, creating a cozy sanctuary.

144

Cranbrook sculptor Carl Milles' "Sunday Morning in Deep Waters," pictured around 1940. Behind this recognizable campus monument stands the Michigan League. Ingalls Mall was later expanded to replace the road shown between the sculpture and the League.

Interior view of the Sports Coliseum in 1940, depicting its structure made of concrete and steel. Located at the corner of Hill Street and Fifth Avenue, the coliseum was used as a skating rink and for ice hockey.

View down Ingalls Mall of Rackham Graduate School and Burton Tower, around 1940.
The Mall bridges the distance between Rackham and the Graduate Library.

Football legend Tom Harmon and actress Anita Louise, his costar in *Harmon of Michigan*, pose next to the Michigan League's "Sunday Morning" fountain in 1941.

Picturesque view of the cloistered Law Quad courtyard, around 1940.

Students taking a break to enjoy the Michigan winter weather during wartime.

Women help in the war effort by selling defense bonds on campus, 1942.

Around 1943, men of Company A take a break from studying to put on a show in the Lydia Mendelssohn Theater, located in the Michigan League building. Company A studied Japanese at the university during this time. The show consisted of two acts and fifteen scenes, written by students.

Company B-4, around 1943, waits for mealtime at the Michigan Union. During the war years, the Union served as dormitory for the Students' Army Training Corps. The union served as a mess hall for about four thousand men and as a dorm for eight hundred.

Students playing a game of cards around 1944. The four aces in the hand at left are going to be tough to beat.

The front of the Romance Languages Building, formerly the University Museum, facing State Street in 1946. The building was razed around 1958 when it was deemed a fire hazard.

Exterior view of the East Quadrangle dormitory between 1940 and 1950. Built in 1940 and opened in 1941, East Quad was used to house enlistees of the Army Air Force, Army Engineers, and Military Intelligence Department during World War II. It switched to being a coed dormitory in 1952.

Early morning sunlight streams through the trees as students walk through the Diag in 1947.

The 1948 UM hockey team, led by coach Vic Heyliger, won the first NCAA Championship Tournament with an 8–4 victory over Dartmouth. Coach Heyliger won a record six national titles and was inducted into the U.S. Hockey Hall of Fame and the University of Michigan Hall of Honor. His UM teams established a 228–61–13 record between 1944 and 1957.

View of the Diag and Ingalls Mall looking towards Rackham from the Graduate library between 1938 and 1948.

The Alice Crocker Lloyd Residence Hall opened in 1949. Alice Crocker Lloyd, class of 1916, was the daughter of the dean of the graduate school, and she was Dean of Women 1930–1950. It was a women-only dorm until 1968 when the Pilot Program (now the Lloyd Hall Scholars Program) moved into the hall.

A drawing class in the
College of Architecture
and Design, 1949.

Architecture & Design class in the Lorch Hall sculpture garden around 1949.

Veteran's Village married-student housing, located near the Coliseum on Hill Street between 1940 and 1955. The post-war enrollment boom (enrollment reached 19,000 in 1946, up from 12,000 after the war in 1945) resulted in a severe housing shortage.

University Terrace was permanent housing built after World War II to meet the increased demand for housing.

Students filing into the stands on Ferry Field, June 11, 1949, for commencement. Both University Hall and Hill Auditorium had previously served as sites for commencement exercises.

167

North University, near State Street, is the site of Hill Auditorium, shown here between 1936 and 1945. The building was constructed in 1913 in order to allow the campus adequate space for convocations and performances. The construction was funded largely by Regent Arthur Hill, in whose honor the building is named. Despite its large size, Hill Auditorium is known for excellent acoustics. Burton Memorial Tower is in the background.

CHANGING TIMES AND BUILDING NEW RESOURCES

(1950–1979)

From 1950 to 1979, the University of Michigan experienced many challenges and achievements. While President Ruthven's tenure had been characterized by the effects of the Great Depression and World War II, incoming President Harlan Hatcher would usher in a new administration, see campus enrollment increase from 17,000 to 41,000 students, and double the number of buildings on campus.

With an ever-growing enrollment came the challenges of providing resources to meet the demand. In 1952, one of the most significant developments was the announcement to purchase three hundred acres that would become North Campus. The buildings of the Memorial Phoenix Project were the first to be built, including the Phoenix Memorial Laboratory and the Ford Nuclear Reactor (the first on a university campus). In the 1960s, North Campus gained the Institute for Science and Technology, the School of Music, dormitories, married student housing, and a commons building.

While the end of the 1940s and the 1950s brought the Cold War and the Space Race—helping to shift the university towards science, technology, and engineering—students' heightened social awareness gave rise to changing attitudes and traditions. Student protest increased in the Sixties. In hopes that a coeducational environment would foster maturity and improve behavior on campus, the Michigan League and Michigan Union became open to both men and women equally. Many residence halls became coed and for the first time, women were allowed to live off-campus.

A shift towards the social sciences saw the completion of the Social Research Institute in 1965. With the changing mood of the country and concerns over civil rights and the Vietnam War, the campus also became more interested in social issues. On October 14, 1960, presidential candidate John F. Kennedy delivered his Peace Corps speech on the Michigan Union steps, introducing his ideas for opportunities for young people to serve their county in new ways. Just four years later, President Lyndon B. Johnson introduced his "Great Society" concept in his commencement address.

In 1974, the University of Michigan's most famous alumnus, Gerald R. Ford, became President of the United States and took steps to heal a nation weary of political scandal. At the close of the 1970s, he returned to campus when the cornerstone was laid for the Gerald R. Ford Presidential Library.

A student march on Lantern Night, between 1950 and 1960. A woman holds up a sign imprinted with the word "Sorosis," the name of a professional women's club founded in New York City whose purpose was to advance the educational and social activities of women and to bring women together. Michigan women had obtained permission to found a collegiate chapter.

Observatory at Portage Lake, 1949. The building of the University Hospital and increasing city lights in Ann Arbor caused the Detroit Observatory to be ineffective. Two hundred acres at Portage Lake, about fifteen miles outside the city, were acquired for new telescopes.

Students at the Michigan League snack bar around 1950.

Students congregate on the steps of Angell Hall between 1951 and 1960. This photo shows the Doric columns and wide expanse of steps chosen by the architect, Albert Kahn. Around this time, new auditoriums for Angell Hall were under construction.

Michigan Stadium aerial view, around 1950. The old wooden bleachers were replaced with steel ones shortly before this picture was taken. The additional seating boosted attendance to 97,239 people from 85,753.

Women students enjoying a meal in the Michigan League dining room, around 1950. The League, which housed several dining rooms and a snack bar, was known for its tasty cuisine.

Economics Building in 1952. The building previously contained the first chemical lab at a state university. The Economics Department occupied the building after the new Chemical Building was built in 1909. The building was consumed by fire on Christmas Eve 1981.

Students stand outside the Waterman gym for registration and orientation in September 1951.

Doctor Elzada Clover, hands
out water lily buds to botany
students. Students (left to right),
Mrs. Benson Murray, New York;
Oka Nichols, Crawfordsville,
Indiana; and Nancy Pridmore,
Oxford, Michigan. Doctor
Clover was one of the first two
women to float the six-hundred-
mile Colorado River on a
botanical expedition to explore
the Grand Canyon in 1938.

Fiftieth Reunion, Class of 1903.

Fielding Yost and women from the Ann Arbor Garden Club examine an exhibit around 1940. Formed in 1929 by Mrs. James Inglis, Mrs. Henry Earhart and Mr. Audrey Tealdi, the Garden Club still exists today. At the time of organization, Tealdi was the Director of the University of Michigan's Nichols Arboretum.

All-American Robert White, hockey team, 1958–1960. White helped win the bronze medal for Canada at the 1956 Olympics in Cortina, Italy.

The announcement of the polio vaccine on April 12, 1955, by President Harlan Hatcher, Professor Thomas Francis, Jonas Salk, and Basil O'Connor (friend and law partner to President Franklin Roosevelt). While Salk attended the University of Michigan to study virology, Thomas Francis taught him vaccine development. After UM he worked at the University of Pittsburgh and the National Foundation for Infantile Paralysis. UM was the largest grant recipient of the foundation.

A view of the gallery in the Martha Cook Dormitory around 1960. Its Gothic and Renaissance style makes this building one of the most striking on campus. The corridor has a floor of marble and red flagged paving, with oak paneled walls. At the end of the gallery is a replica of the statue of the Venus de Milo.

John F. Kennedy proposes the Peace Corps on the Michigan Union steps at 2:00 a.m., October 14, 1960. Then-Senator Kennedy began this unprepared speech by saying "I want to express my thanks to you, as a graduate of the Michigan of the East, Harvard University." He continued the speech by challenging students to commit to several years of public service.

The West Physics Building burns during its demolition in 1966. Irving Kane and Allen B. Pond were the architects of the building, constructed in 1887 to meet enrollment increases following the Civil War. It was destroyed to make room for construction of the New Library.

Fire during demolition of
the West Physics Building
in 1966. In the background
is the Clements Library.

The Anthropology faculty gathered for a party honoring a Mrs. Burd, a secretary who left her position in 1964 after many years of service. Pictured standing, left to right, are Leslie A. White, Mervyn Meggitt, Norma Diamond, Horace Miner, J. N. Spuhler, Aram Yengoyan, and Ernst Goldschmidt. Seated are James B. Griffin, Frank Livingstone, Volney H. Jones, Robert Burns, and Eric Wolf, with Elman Service reclining.

The Cube, shown here, around 1968. Located in Regents Plaza, this gift from the Class of 1965 spins on its axis when you push it. The Cube's designer, Tony Rosenthal, was a graduate of the class of 1936. Campus legend says that the president gives it a ceremonial push each morning on the way to his office in order to get the university under way.

191

Gerald Ford stands with Coach Bo Schembechler at football practice, 1972. Ford's football jersey, number 48, was retired at the October 1994 Michigan State game. Schembechler was UM's winningest head coach (1967–1989), with a 194–48–5 record, and served as director of athletics, 1988–1990.

University graduate Maxine (Micki) King shown with her gold medal from the 1972 Munich Olympic Games. She won the gold medal in the three-meter dive and placed fifth in platform diving. While at Michigan, King was twice All-American goalie for the water polo team. She went on to coach at the Unites States Military Academy.

Three women perform
modern dance, 1952.

President Robben Wright Fleming (1968–1979) at a student demonstration at noon, June 18, 1969. Fleming was known for letting students air grievances, thereby gaining their trust and averting the problems many other universities experienced during those turbulent times.

McMath-Hulbert Observatory, located at Lake Angelus (near Pontiac) was founded by businessman Francis C. McMath, his son Robert R. McMath, and Judge Henry S. Hulbert. Director of the Astronomy Department, Ralph H. Curtiss, became interested when he saw moving pictures of the moon taken at the observatory in 1928. The property was deeded to the university in 1939.

Harlan Hatcher (UM President), Walker Cisler (President, Detroit Edison Company), Dean Sawyer (Dean of Rackham and the Director of the Michigan Memorial Phoenix Project) Chester Lang (VP, General Electric), and George Romney (President, American Motors Corporation and later governor) were among those present for the Phoenix Project Memorial Laboratory dedication on Atom Day, June 9, 1955. The laboratory is a working memorial to University members who lost their lives in World War II and is dedicated to developing peaceful uses for nuclear technology.

Protest, late 1960s. View from the Graduate Library steps looking down Ingalls Mall to Rackham. The 1960s saw a marked increase in demonstrations as students protested regarding the Vietnam War, student rights, and minority issues on campus.

Gerald Ford at the cornerstone-laying ceremony for the Gerald R. Ford Presidential Library on North Campus, 1979. The library's collection includes material on foreign relations, domestic issues, and politics during the Cold War era, as well as information on Ford's life and presidency. The library is a part of National Archives and Records Administration's presidential library system.

Notes on the Photographs

These notes, listed by page number, attempt to include all aspects known of the photographs. Each of the photographs is identified by the page number, photograph's title or description, photographer and collection, archive, and call or box number when applicable. Although every attempt was made to collect all available data, in some cases complete data was unavailable due to the age and condition of some of the photographs and records.

27 **ANATOMICAL LABORATORY**
Bentley Historical Library,
University of Michigan
BL002089

28 **DISSECTING ROOM**
Bentley Historical Library,
University of Michigan
BL002091

29 **STATE STREET**
Bentley Historical Library,
University of Michigan
BL001941

30 **ALICE HAMILTON**
Bentley Historical Library,
University of Michigan
BL002078

31 **CHEMISTRY LECTURE**
Bentley Historical Library,
University of Michigan
BL002006

32 **WATERMAN GYMNASIUM**
Bentley Historical Library,
University of Michigan
BL004595

33 **LAW BUILDING**
Bentley Historical Library,
University of Michigan
BL004346

34 **FOOTBALL PLAYERS**
Bentley Historical Library,
University of Michigan
BL000192

35 **UNIVERSITY HOSPITAL**
Bentley Historical Library,
University of Michigan
BL005102

36 **LOUIS ELBEL**
Bentley Historical Library,
University of Michigan
BL003801

38 **THE "LAWS"**
Bentley Historical Library,
University of Michigan
BL003702

39 **BEN FRANKLIN STATUE**
Bentley Historical Library,
University of Michigan
BL004494

40 **REGENTS FIELD**
Bentley Historical Library,
University of Michigan
BL001092

42 **SENIOR SWING OUT**
Bentley Historical Library,
University of Michigan
BL003703

43 **ARCHIE HAHN**
Bentley Historical Library,
University of Michigan
BL001086

44 **CHEMISTRY LAB**
Bentley Historical Library,
University of Michigan
BL004185

45 **UNIVERSITY HALL**
Bentley Historical Library,
University of Michigan
BL004548

46 **FIELD HOCKEY**
Bentley Historical Library,
University of Michigan
BL001139

47 **AESTHETIC DANCING**
Bentley Historical Library,
University of Michigan
BL006857

48 **STUDENTS RELAXING**
Bentley Historical Library,
University of Michigan
BL000237

49 **ANATOMICAL LAB**
Bentley Historical Library,
University of Michigan
BL001790

50 **FERRY FIELD**
Bentley Historical Library,
University of Michigan
BL000250

51 **GENERAL LIBRARY**
Bentley Historical Library,
University of Michigan
BL005194

52 **PUSH BALL**
Bentley Historical Library,
University of Michigan
BL003697

53 **JUDGE GRANT**
Bentley Historical Library,
University of Michigan
BL001780

54 **WOMEN'S BASKETBALL**
Bentley Historical Library,
University of Michigan
BL000266

55 **DAVE ALLERDICE**
Bentley Historical Library,
University of Michigan
BL001437

56 **BARBOUR GYMNASIUM**
Bentley Historical Library,
University of Michigan
BL004597

57 **FERRY FIELD**
Bentley Historical Library,
University of Michigan
BL001118

58 **THE DIAG**
Bentley Historical Library,
University of Michigan
BL001911

59 **BARBOUR GYMNASIUM**
Bentley Historical Library,
University of Michigan
BL001137

60 **SENIOR WOMEN**
Bentley Historical Library,
University of Michigan
BL003681

61 **J-HOP**
Bentley Historical Library,
University of Michigan
BL003691

62 **GENERAL LIBRARY**
Bentley Historical Library,
University of Michigan
BL005207

64 **UNION CLUBHOUSE**
Bentley Historical Library,
University of Michigan
BL004683

65 **FUNERAL PROCESSION**
Bentley Historical Library,
University of Michigan
BL000111

146 SPORTS COLESIUM
Bentley Historical Library,
University of Michigan
BL004107

147 BURTON TOWER
Bentley Historical Library,
University of Michigan
BL004060

148 "SUNDAY MORNING"
Bentley Historical Library,
University of Michigan
BL001078

149 LAW QUAD COURTYARD
Bentley Historical Library,
University of Michigan
BL005152

150 SNOWBALL FIGHT
Bentley Historical Library,
University of Michigan
BL003723

151 SOLDIERS STUDYING
Bentley Historical Library,
University of Michigan
BL000180

152 SELLING WAR BONDS
Bentley Historical Library,
University of Michigan
BL005309

153 COMPANY A SHOW
Bentley Historical Library,
University of Michigan
BL003846

154 COMPANY B-4
Bentley Historical Library,
University of Michigan
BL003838

155 FOUR ACES
Bentley Historical Library,
University of Michigan
BL003805

156 ROMANCE LANGUAGES
Bentley Historical Library,
University of Michigan
BL004449

157 EAST QUADRANGLE
Bentley Historical Library,
University of Michigan
BL004155

158 EARLY MORNING
Bentley Historical Library,
University of Michigan
BL000243

159 UM HOCKEY TEAM
Bentley Historical Library,
University of Michigan
BL003076

160 INGALLS MALL
Bentley Historical Library,
University of Michigan
BL001906

161 RESIDENCE HALL
Bentley Historical Library,
University of Michigan
BL001777

162 DRAWING CLASS
Bentley Historical Library,
University of Michigan
BL000246

163 SCULPTURE GARDEN
Bentley Historical Library,
University of Michigan
BL005241

164 VETERAN'S VILLAGE
Bentley Historical Library,
University of Michigan
BL004585

165 UNIVERSITY TERRACE
Bentley Historical Library,
University of Michigan
BL004582

166 COMMENCEMENT, 1949
Bentley Historical Library,
University of Michigan
BL000240

168 HILL AUDITORIUM
Bentley Historical Library,
University of Michigan
BL005046

170 STUDENT MARCH
Bentley Historical Library,
University of Michigan
BL003700

171 OBSERVATORY
Bentley Historical Library,
University of Michigan
BL001701

172 SNACK BAR
Bentley Historical Library,
University of Michigan
BL004761

173 ANGELL HALL
Bentley Historical Library,
University of Michigan
BL001798

174 MICHIGAN STADIUM
Bentley Historical Library,
University of Michigan
BL004766

175 DINING ROOM
Bentley Historical Library,
University of Michigan
BL004760

176 ECONOMICS BUILDING
Bentley Historical Library,
University of Michigan
BL004176

177 REGISTRATION
Bentley Historical Library,
University of Michigan
BL000236

178 DOCTOR CLOVER
Bentley Historical Library,
University of Michigan
BL000245

180 FIFTIETH REUNION
Bentley Historical Library,
University of Michigan
BL003656

181 GARDEN CLUB
Bentley Historical Library,
University of Michigan
BL005304

182 ROBERT WHITE
Bentley Historical Library,
University of Michigan
BL003245

183 POLIO VACCINE
Bentley Historical Library,
University of Michigan
BL006836

184 MARTHA COOK DORM
Bentley Historical Library,
University of Michigan
BL000062